W9-BKV-720

CHICAGO PUBLIC LIBRARY
HEGEWISCH BRANCH
3048 E. 130TH ST.

DISCARD

Exploremos la galaxia/Exploring the Galaxy

Urano/Uranus

por/by Thomas K. Adamson

Traducción/Translation: Martín Luis Guzmán Ferrer, Ph.D.
Editor Consultor/Consulting Editor: Dra. Gail Saunders-Smith

James Gerard, Consultant
Aerospace Education Specialist, NASA
Kennedy Space Center, Florida

Capstone
press

Mankato, Minnesota

Pebble Plus is published by Capstone Press
151 Good Counsel Drive, P.O. Box 669, Mankato, Minnesota 56002
http://www.capstone-press.com

Copyright © 2006 by Capstone Press. All rights reserved.
No part of this publication may be reproduced in whole or in part, or stored in a retrieval system, or transmitted in any form or by any means, electronic, mechanical, photocopying, recording, or otherwise, without written permission of the publisher.
For information regarding permission, write to Capstone Press,
151 Good Counsel Drive, P.O. Box 669, Dept. R, Mankato, Minnesota 56002.
Printed in the United States of America

1 2 3 4 5 6 11 10 09 08 07 06

Library of Congress Cataloging-in-Publication Data
Adamson, Thomas K.
   [Uranus. Spanish & English]
   Urano = Uranus / by Thomas K. Adamson.
   p. cm.—(Pebble plus: Exploremos la galaxia = Exploring the galaxy)
   English and Spanish.
   Includes index.
   ISBN-13: 978-0-7368-5885-4 (hardcover)
   ISBN-10: 0-7368-5885-7 (hardcover)
   1. Uranus (Planet)—Juvenile literature. I. Title: Uranus. II. Title. III. Series.
QB681.A3318 2005
523.47—dc22   2005019045

Summary: Simple text and photographs describe the planet Uranus.

Editorial Credits
Mari C. Schuh, editor; Kia Adams, designer; Alta Schaffer, photo researcher; Eida del Risco, Spanish copy editor; Jenny Marks, bilingual editor

Photo Credits
Digital Vision, 5 (Venus)
NASA, 4 (Pluto), 7, 11, 13, 15, 17, 19, 21; JPL, 5 (Jupiter); JPL/Caltech, cover, 1, 5 (Uranus), 9 (Uranus)
PhotoDisc Inc., 4 (Neptune), 5 (Earth, Sun, Mars, Mercury, Saturn), 9 (Earth)

Note: Some of the images in this book are false-color images that use artificial colors to enhance planet features.

Note to Parents and Teachers

The Exploremos la galaxia/Exploring the Galaxy series supports national standards related to earth and space science. This book describes Uranus in both English and Spanish. The photographs support early readers and language learners in understanding the text. Repetition of words and phrases helps early readers and language learners learn new words. This book also introduces early readers to subject-specific vocabulary words, which are defined in the Glossary section. Early readers may need assistance to read some words and to use the Table of Contents, Glossary, Internet Sites, and Index sections of the book.

CHICAGO PUBLIC LIBRARY
HEGEWISCH BRANCH
3048 E. 130TH ST.   602

R0407577125

Table of Contents

Tabla de contenidos

Uranus

Uranus is the seventh planet from the Sun. Uranus and the other planets move around the Sun.

Urano

Urano es el séptimo planeta a partir del Sol. Urano y los demás planetas se mueven alrededor del Sol.

The Solar System/El sistema solar

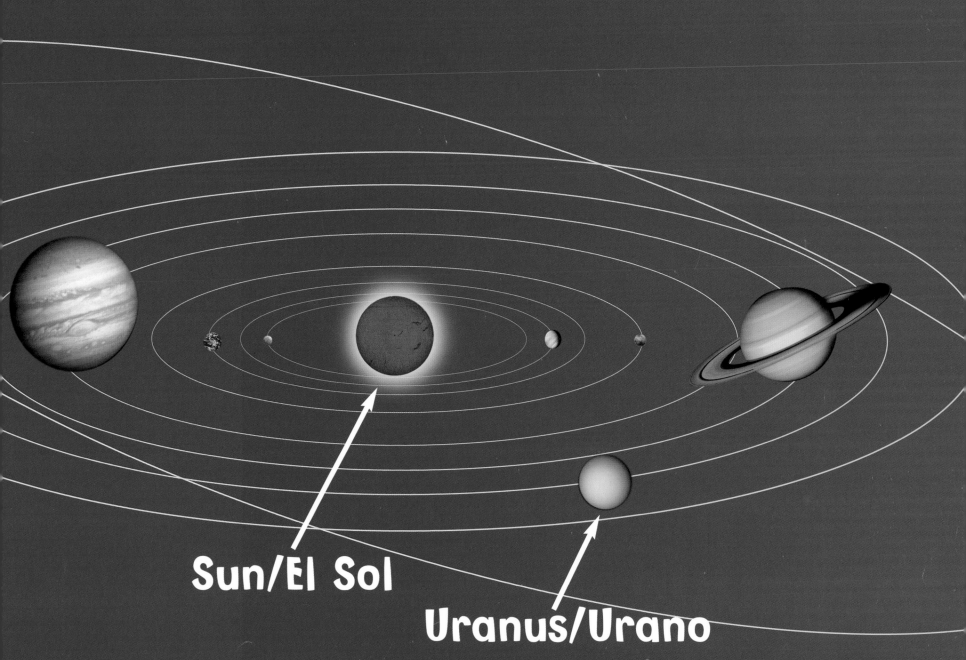

Sun/El Sol

Uranus/Urano

Most planets spin like
a top as they move around
the Sun. But Uranus spins
on its side.

La mayoría de los planetas
giran como un trompo mientras
se mueven alrededor del Sol.
Pero Urano gira de lado.

Uranus is the third largest
planet. Uranus is four times
wider than Earth.

Urano es el tercer planeta
más grande. Urano es cuatro
veces más ancho que la Tierra.

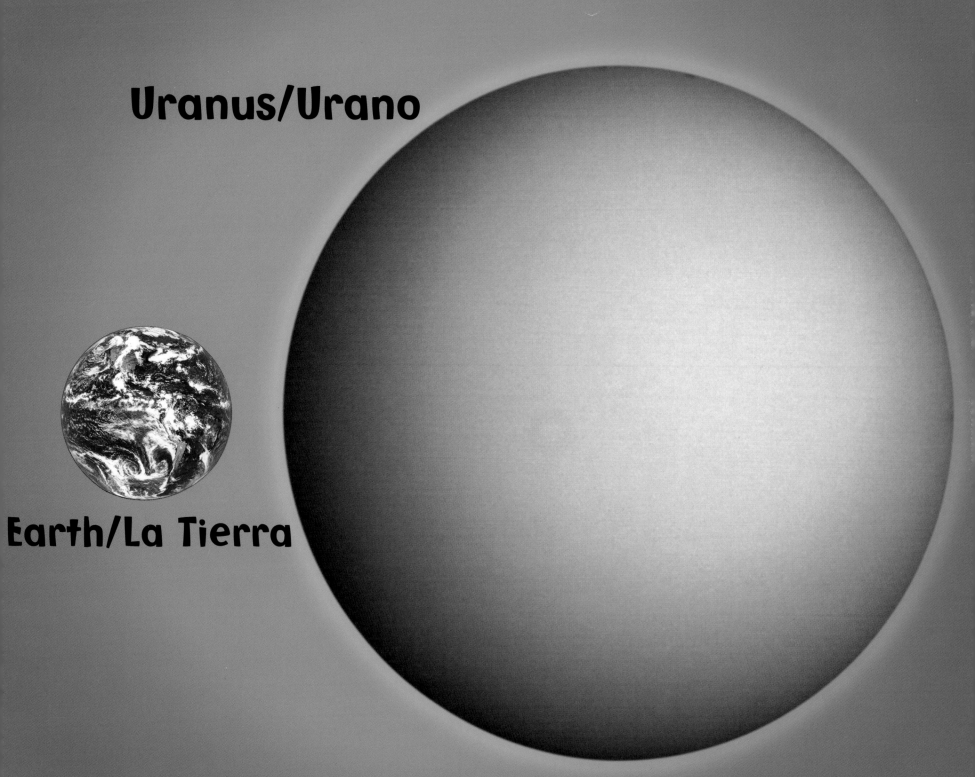

Uranus/Urano

Earth/La Tierra

Moons

At least 21 moons move around Uranus. Earth has one moon.

Lunas

Por lo menos 21 lunas se mueven alrededor de Urano. La Tierra sólo tiene una luna.

one of Uranus' moons
una de las lunas de Urano

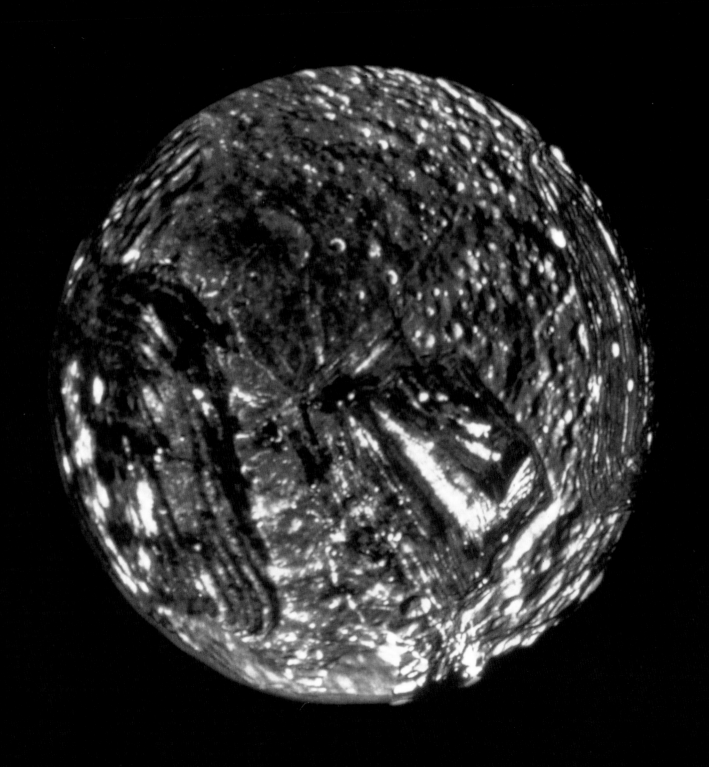

Features

Uranus is a big ball of
clouds, gases, and liquid.
Uranus is called a gas giant.

Características

Urano es una bola enorme
de nubes, gases y líquidos.
Urano es un gigante gaseoso.

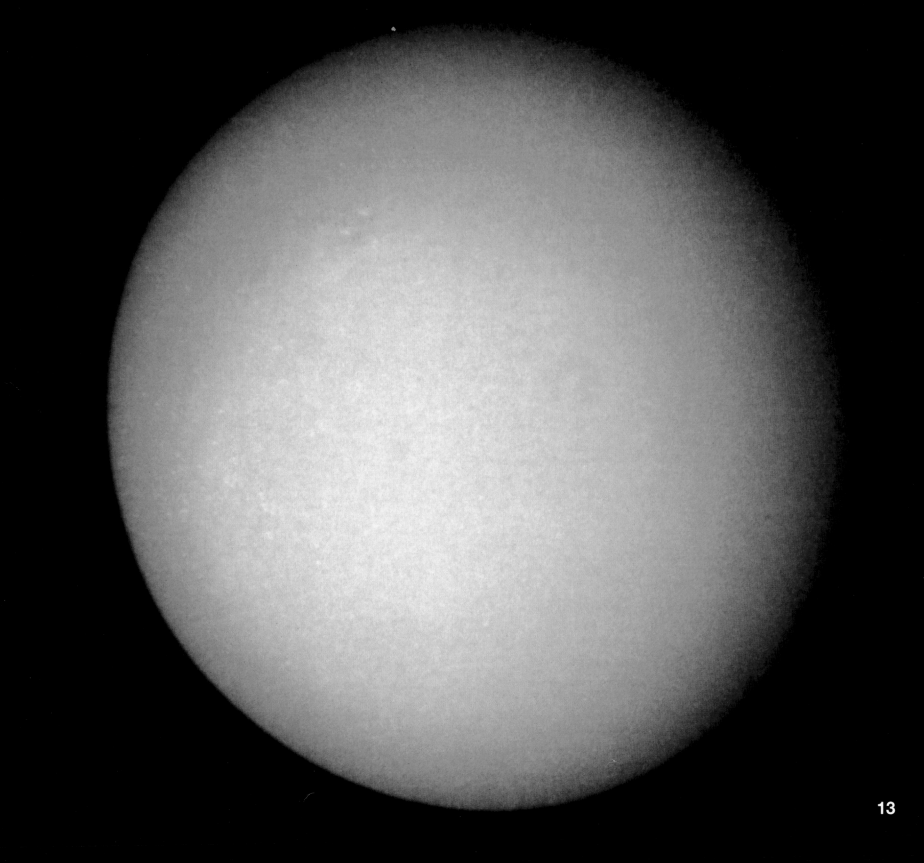

13

Clouds cover Uranus.
The clouds give Uranus
a blue color.

Las nubes cubren a Urano.
Las nubes le dan a Urano
un color azul.

Uranus has 11 dark rings
around it. The thin rings
are made of rock and dust.

Urano tiene 11 anillos
oscuros a su alrededor.
Los finos anillos están
hechos de roca y polvo.

People and Uranus

Uranus does not have a solid surface. A spacecraft could not land on Uranus. People could not walk on Uranus.

La gente y Urano

Urano no tiene una superficie sólida. Una nave espacial no podría aterrizar en Urano. La gente no podría caminar en Urano.

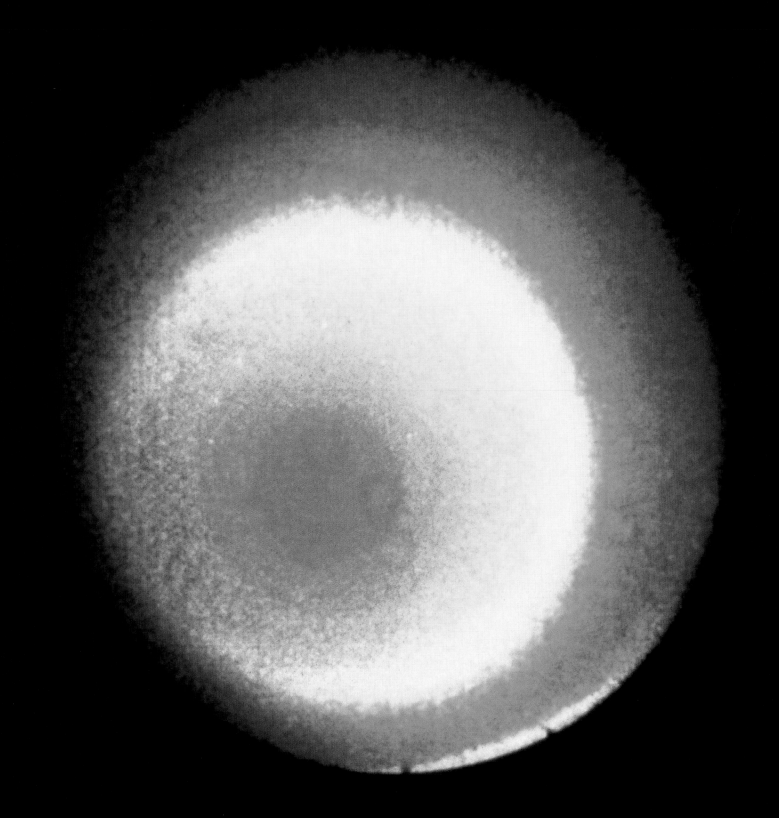

People on Earth cannot
easily see Uranus without
a telescope. Uranus is
too far away.

La gente no puede ver
fácilmente a Urano sin
un telescopio. Urano está
demasiado lejos.

Glossary

gas—a substance, such as air, that spreads to fill any space that holds it

moon—an object that moves around a planet; Cordelia, Ophelia, Bianca, and Cressida are the moons closest to Uranus.

planet—a large object that moves around the Sun; Uranus is the third largest planet; only Jupiter and Saturn are larger than Uranus.

spacecraft—a vehicle that is used to travel in space

Sun—the star that the planets move around; the Sun provides light and heat for the planets.

telescope—a tool people use to look at planets and other objects in space; telescopes make planets and other objects look closer than they really are.

Glosario

gas—una sustancia, como el aire, que se extiende hasta llenar el espacio que la contiene

luna—un objeto que se mueve alrededor de un planeta; Cordelia, Ofelia, Blanca y Cressida son las lunas más cercanas a Urano.

nave espacial—un vehículo que se usa para viajar en el espacio

planeta—un objeto grande que se mueve alrededor del Sol; Urano es el tercer planeta más grande; sólo Júpiter y Saturno son más grandes que Urano.

Sol—la estrella alrededor de la cual se mueven los planetas; el Sol proporciona luz y calor a los planetas.

telescopio—un instrumento que la gente usa para ver planetas y otros objetos en el espacio; los telescopios hacen que los planetas y otros objetos se vean más cerca de lo que están.

Internet Sites

Do you want to find out more about Uranus and the solar system? Let FactHound, our fact-finding hound dog, do the research for you.

Here's how:

1) Visit *www.facthound.com*

2) Type in the **Book ID** number: 073682118X

3) Click on **FETCH IT.**

FactHound will fetch Internet sites picked by our editors just for you!

Sitios de Internet

¿Quieres saber más sobre Urano y el sistema solar? Deja que FactHound, nuestro perro sabueso, haga la investigación por ti.

Así:

1) Ve a **www.facthound.com**

2) Teclea el número ID del libro: **073682118X**

3) Clic en **FETCH IT.**

¡Facthound buscará en los sitios de Internet que han seleccionado nuestros editores sólo para ti!

Index

Índice